D0236591

LEH

SRINAGAR

LADAKH

KASHMIR

PESHAWAR

HIMALAYAS

TIBET

LHASA

LAHORE

QUETTA

DELHI

ISTAN

PAKISTAN

KATHMANDU

NEPAL

INDIA

CALCUTTA

PILGRIMAGE

PAUL OSBORNE

PILGRIMAGE

An artist's journey from Mount Athos to Tibet

GEORGE
PHILIP

This book is copyrighted under the Berne
Convention. All rights reserved. Apart from any fair
dealing for the purpose of private study, research,
criticism or review, as permitted under the
Copyright Act, 1956, no part of this publication may
be reproduced, stored in a retrieval system, or
transmitted in any form or by any means, electronic,
electrical, chemical, mechanical, optical,
photocopying, recording, or otherwise, without
prior written permission. All enquiries should be
addressed to the Publishers.

British Library Cataloguing in Publication Data

Osborne, Paul 1958–
    Pilgrimage: an artist's journey from Mount Athos to Tibet.
    1. South Asia. Description & travel
    I. Title
    915.4' 0452

ISBN 0-540-01200-9

This edition Copyright © 1989 by Toucan Books Limited

Illustrations Copyright © 1989 by Paul Osborne

First published by George Philip Ltd,
59 Grosvenor Street, London W1X 9DA

Typeset by Florencetype Ltd, Kewstoke, Avon
Printed and bound in West Germany

Contents

Introduction

WILLIAM SIMPSON, that celebrated Victorian artist-traveller, is on record as saying that as an artist he felt at times that he was not just seeing for himself alone, but for others – some as yet unborn – who would follow. He had in mind the readers of the *Illustrated London News*, the journal for which he worked as a Special Artist for much of his long life. Its readers followed his adventures throughout the world as keenly as he enjoyed depicting them.

There can be little doubt that Paul Osborne's dedication and talent place him in such company – in a tradition which not only includes Simpson, but also George Chinnery, Thomas and William Daniell, Edward Lear and before them, William Coke-Smyth, William Hodges, John Sykes and John Webber, who accompanied the expeditions which explored the uncharted horizons of the Atlantic and the Pacific as draughtsmen and topographical watercolourists for the East India Company and the Admiralty.

Like those artists, Osborne's dedication is highly motivated and rests firmly on both a physical and intellectual foundation. This has enabled him to undertake the formidable feats of endurance which invariably face such artists. The long and exhausting journeys through chilly nights as well as in the heat of tropical days; the tramping through forests and the scaling of vertiginous heights to obtain the right vantage point essential for making panoramic configurations of rock, sea and sky. And not to forget the infinite patience necessary to cope with the sometimes unwelcome curiosity of bewhiskered tribesmen, persistent beggars and nimble children.

Stylistically too, Osborne's work reflects the influence of several of the artists I have mentioned, especially Simpson and Lear. By and large he paints what he sees, but does so with a sure sense of the spirit of a given place. If, at times, his figures tend to be cyphers, we are after all looking through a sketchbook – always a vital and searching means of understanding *what* is going on, of perhaps intensifying the eternal, rather than observing the ephemeral.

For the artist-traveller, art – to paraphrase the poet Arthur Symons – begins when the artist wishes to immortalise the most vivid moment he has lived. Osborne on his pilgrimage discovered many such moments in the remotest of mountain fastnesses, the last strongholds of religious faiths reaching back to half-forgotten epochs. In themselves his images possess an almost kinetic quality in that they reflect his mounting excitement and sense of wonder as one extraordinary visual experience followed another. My own favourites include the panoramic view of the Royal Palace at Leh (Ladakh) on pages 62–63 with the Himalaya in the distant background; climaxing with the superbly composed view of the Potala at Lhasa (Tibet) on pages 94–95. In such watercolour studies, one senses that the sheer exoticism of the subjects extended the artist.

In his reflective account of his odyssey, Paul Osborne endearingly admits to making the occasional mistake to which all artist-travellers are prone, simply because their thoughts are elsewhere. He places his portfolio of precious paper and folding easel on the roof of a truck. Inevitably, both fall off into a stream, half the paper is soaked; a vital part of the easel is missing. My own mistake on one recent journey was checking-in a bulging portfolio of completed drawings simply because I had so much to carry on the plane. But instead of accompanying me on the same aircraft from Cuba to Jamaica, it went on to Nicaragua instead! Yet people always like artists and help us whenever possible. The missing part of Osborne's easel was found by a concerned Kashmiri woman. My portfolio eventually turned up in Haiti ten days later through the courtesy of a concerned airline employee.

Paul Osborne' pilgrimage was a watershed, a breakthrough for his future as a documentary artist. I look forward to seeing the fruits of his next project with great interest. Meanwhile, here is impressive evidence that the peculiarly British tradition of the globe-trotting artist with the roving eye remains very much alive. Such an artist is a rare bird these days, but there are signs that in the person of Paul Osborne he may well have staged a comeback.

Paul Hogarth

April 1989

It was April in 1986.
I was irresistibly drawn to the journey overland to the East,
not only to see what was on the other side of the horizon,
but to trace a line back to something of our roots, a road of discovery,
with an inner sense as much as an outer.
So I found myself on the deck of a boat leaving England,
with an easel, a generous supply of paper and my bags full of paints.
I spent more than a year travelling across Asia to Lhasa.
These are the paintings I made on that journey.

Mount Athos: The Holy Mountain

AS I TOOK the ferry from mainland Greece to Mount Athos, the boat's wake rippled across a smooth sea, and the Holy Mountain of Athos stood ahead in misty blue relief. Gradually, as we came closer and the mist cleared a little, I began to make out the first monasteries above the shore, appearing half-hidden in the trees, and, at the water's edge, their 'arsenals', medieval gateways to an older world. Nothing had changed since Edward Lear had come to paint in Athos. The boat landed at Daphni, the little port, and the monks and I climbed on to an ancient bus that rattled and rumbled its way laboriously uphill to Karyes, the capital.

The next morning I walked down the path on the eastern side, through woods full of sunlight and birdsong, with ruined monasteries here and there, calling out to be painted; then down to Stavronikita, perching on its cliff edge by the sea. I had never seen anything like the beauty of this place, the buildings sitting in the landscape in a way that I had always been searching for but had only ever found in glimpses. It is something to do with the materials – stone and wood, everything taken from the place itself – and the way in which these monasteries, like little walled towns, are sited, in a hollow or on a pinnacle, to harmonise with the geography around them. But it is more than that. The whole mountain is sacred, and these buildings have nothing but a sacred purpose themselves. I began to see the kind of landscape that used to exist in the rest of Europe, where the roads and paths made by man followed the shapes of the land, where life was slower, and where the buildings seemed to form part of the natural world.

I walked down the coast to Ivieron, with its echoing empty corridors and its framed engravings on the walls, and stayed the night there. I spent most of the following day in Karakallou, the next monastery down the coast, high up on the hillside, sipping sweet black coffee and ouzo, in a window seat looking out over the tree tops to the sea, not a boat in sight, only the swallows darting out into the wide blue space, and the sound of the wind.

Athos is a monastic community, one of the last pockets of Byzantine culture, dedicated to devotion and prayer, to a form of worship very different from the one I had known. It was this that had drawn me there, to experience the Orthodox monastic way of life, and to search for the spiritual source of the icons. I was already familiar with the styles of iconography, but it is not until the paintings are seen in context that they can take on their true meaning. To be surrounded by incense and candles, the golden halos of the saints glittering in the shadows, is to be reminded that it is the holy ceremony which gives the icons their significance. The spirit is instilled into the image by the faith and devotion of the monks, as they bow three times to the icon of the saint of the day. The ceremonies give an insight into the reason for an icon's existence – to be the embodiment of a spiritual ideal, literally a 'realization'.

The rhythm of prayer, the sincerity of the monks' devotions and the pattern of holy ritual are all part of one thing. Through them, the icons, the architecture and the whole mountain are all dedicated to God and the glory of his creation. To this end the iconographer remains anonymous, since it is not his own personality that needs to be expressed, but rather a spiritual vision that has been passed down for centuries. Fashion and style matter little, since what is portrayed in an icon is timeless, tapping a deeper undercurrent than personal expression: the visible form of the Invisible.

After a long walk through the oak forests, past mountain streams, all of them cold from the summit of Athos, I arrived on tired feet at Megista Lavra, the largest and oldest of the monasteries, founded in the tenth century. It was Lent and the food was sparse but welcome: dark cabbage soup, with a plate of olives and half a decanter of wine from the monastery's own vineyards. I had missed the main meal of the day and sat in a small side-room at a wooden table looking out to sea with a pair of pre-war binoculars. The next day I ate with the monks at the marble tables of the refectory, where the walls are covered in tall saints with golden halos against a pure blue ground. In the half-dome apse above the abbot's table, Christ reigns, flanked by John the Baptist and the Virgin Mary. On one of the sidewalls of an adjoining room is a very large painting of the Last Judgement. A flowing river of fire is slashed across it, dividing the saved from the damned.

I left most of Lavra unexplored to continue my walk, on a rocky path up the western coast to Dionyssiou, where the monks called me *agiographos*, the saint painter, ensured that I had everything I needed while painting and allowed me to stay an extra day to paint the astonishing icons of the Revelation outside the Refectory.

My time was running out and in the morning I caught the boat up the coast to Daphni and then walked up past the near-deserted buildings of Panteleimonos, a Russian monastery where the strands of white curtains blew through the broken windows, and then on to Dochiariou where I painted until the sun dropped under the Aegean. In the evening a monk showed me some of the painted walls – a long row of saints included one he described as 'the Wise Prince from the East', said to be the Buddha. He is painted in the traditional Byzantine way, a merging of East and West. Opposite the line of saints is a row of beautiful windows looking out on to the sea, each alcove painted with different flowers and plants. The dedication and intensity of feeling in the painting extended to every tiny part of the work. There seemed to be as much love put into simple decoration as into the face of the Divine.

That evening I waited late into the night to hear the singing in the church, sitting in the high wooden seats, as bats flitted round in the candlelit gloom and the light glinted off golden candlesticks, the iconostasis and the icons on the walls around us. I slept that night in a white room with the sound of the sea coming in through the open windows and a gentle breeze brushing through the cypresses and orange trees. A nightingale sang and Venus shone brilliant-white through the window.

The next day the clouds and rain came in as I left on the ferry back to the mainland. I was sorry to leave and knew I would return one day.

12   *Mount Athos from the capital, Karyes. April 23rd 1986*

13

14   *Icons in the church of the Protaton, Karyes. April 23rd 1986*

15

16

Entrance to the monastery of Stavronikita. April 24th 1986 17

18 *Monastery of Karakallou, from the tower. April 25th 1986*

19

20

Near the southern tip of Mount Athos. April 27th 1986   21

22   *Monastery of Dionyssiou: wall paintings from the Book of Revelation outside the refectory. April 28th 1986*

24

The Russian monastery of Pantelemnonos. April 29th 1986   25

26.

Monastery of Dochiariou, late afternoon. April 29th 1986   27

30   *Istanbul from the Galata Bridge: the Golden Horn. May 12th 1986*

31

32

Agia Sophia and the Blue Mosque from my hotel window. May 14th 1986   33

Topkapi Palace, Istanbul: the Sultan's Quarters. May 15th 1986   35

Mardin, eastern Turkey, at dawn. June 18th 1986   37

Mar Gabriel, Syriac Orthodox Monastery, eastern Turkey. June 25th 1986   39

The landscape around Mar Gabriel at dusk. June 28th 1986 41

42

The Church of the Holy Cross, Akdamar, Lake Van, eastern Turkey. July 3rd 1986   43

44   *Mount Ararat from Doğubeyazit, eastern Turkey. July 5th 1986*

45

The vegetable market in Peshawar, Pakistan. July 26th 1986 47

48

Badshahi Mosque from the fort, Lahore, Pakistan. August 6th 1986 49

Ladakh: into the Mountains

I WAS ON A BUS northwards to Kashmir, to escape the heat and head for the hills. 'He who goes to the hills goes to his mother.' How to describe what it meant to be going into the Himalaya? It was the paramount destination of my journey, my reason for coming to Asia at all. A feeling deeper than expectation, something closer to a spiritual need, to discover the teachings of the East, the source of the Holy Ganges, the realm of Buddhism, where the air is clear and cool.

We drove up into the heavily wooded hills, scattered with wooden huts, climbing all the time, grinding the gears, until at last at the top, at the far end of a tunnel which pierces the crest of the range, the Vale of Kashmir stretched out green and calm in front of us. Dropping to the valley floor, then on down long straight avenues of silver birch and poplar, to Srinagar. Despite the usual frantic bustle and worries on arriving in a city, it turned out to be a slow and easy place, a city of wooden boats and wooden latticed windows, filled with the slow motion of the boats gliding over the lake, or between the houses and trees and under the bridges.

I managed to get a lift early one morning from a young Sikh taking a truck to Ladakh. He was a manic driver, trying to overtake everything even if there was no room on the road. As we careered around one bend, I distinctly heard my easel and folder fall off the roof. 'STOP!' I shouted and ran back to get them. Both had fallen into a stream – half the paper inside was soaked, and pieces of the easel were missing. I found them all but one. The truck driver was sitting up in his cab, hooting the horn. After many long minutes of searching, the missing part was found by a Kashmiri woman, wading barefoot into the stream. I gave her 10 rupees and thanked her as best I could.

We drove on in the multicolour truck, up into an Alpine region, all pines and rocky streams and houses with slate roofs like Swiss chalets. Up to Sonamarg, the Golden Valley, a resting spot before the pass, and a very lovely place, all smooth grassy flanks and sheep, and swathes of snow higher under the beautiful bright sunlight.

We drove on for two days. All along the way I kept seeing mountain formations I wanted to paint. But we couldn't stop and the truck was too bumpy even to use the small sketchbook. We reached Mulbekh, coming to a halt near the huge stone figure of the Buddha Maitreya, his hand raised, surrounded by the high, jagged peaks of the mountains, as if in welcome to all travellers entering this other world.

The road went on, sometimes across bleak and windswept plateaux, sometimes along the edge of a steep rock face, before winding down to the depths of a valley, running like a green band between the red, brown and yellow flanks of the mountains, streaked in purple.

For most of the second day of this journey I sat in the tool box above the driver's cab, the best place from which to see the passing land. Children by the roadside and by the short, white, flat-topped buildings, sold us large bags of ripe apricots for a few rupees. A Ladakhi sat up on the top with me, singing songs to the air and sky, or to his home, and danced with his hands and fingers in sinuous rhythmic patterns, as the truck rumbled into Leh valley. We reached Leh in the middle of the night, the town lying around us, pitch dark and mysterious.

Leh is high, cool and dry, and everything smelled and tasted different. It has a medieval quality, a place filled with the sense of ancient continuity. The rough stone and mud buildings are muddled together at the foot of the palace walls and riddled with tiny pathways and tunnels. Lines of prayer flags blow in the constant wind, printed with the image of the Wind Horse, hundreds of them joining hilltops or the corners of roofs. From the old flags the image has faded, absorbed away by the sun and wind. The stupas crumble back into the land; the cairns of stones grow naturally out of the rocks around them. All nature seems to be partaking in the religion of this place. The stupas symbolise the elements in their very shape: rising from the cube of earth as the foundation, through the sphere of water, the cone of fire and the crescent of air to the crowning twist of ether. And the mani stones, carved with the Tibetan 'Om Mani Padme Hum', roughly translated as 'Hail to the jewel in the heart of the lotus', are piled along the mani walls. The stone is instilled with a sacredness that touches a deep primaeval chord within. At night the moon was large, with concentric rings of coloured light around it, the seas clearly visible on its surface. Four planets – Jupiter, Mars, Venus and Saturn – each in its own colours, hung above the mountains where the ice and snow reflected the moonlight.

52

Dal Lake, from the Hindu Temple, Srinagar, Kashmir. August 21st 1986   53

54   *Buddha painted on rock face, Leh, Ladakh. August 27th 1986*

56   *Tsemo Gompa and prayer flags near Leh. September 3rd 1986*

57

Kitchen of the Palace View Kidar Hotel, Leh. September 4th 1986   59

60   *Interior of the Shrine Room, Royal Palace, Leh. September 7th 1986*

62

Royal Palace, Leh, from the old town. September 9th 1986   63

The Ladakhi monasteries inside are dark and densely packed with wall paintings, cloth hangings and cases of images, where many small gold Buddhas are wrapped up like dolls, barely visible by butterlamp. The paintings on the walls flicker in the light. Wrathful deities trample on Ignorance. Screaming wild figures in red and blue are entwined with their consorts. The smell is of yak-butter and age. Above all this is the distant, refined smile of the reserved Buddha, implying some hidden understanding of the seeming chaos of our ordinary lives.

I spent many weeks at the monastery of Sankar Gompa in Leh, studying the wall paintings. I breathed the atmosphere surrounding the place, as the wind blew cool from the mountains, and watched the slow change of the season towards Autumn. In one of the temples a solitary monk mumbled away in a corner, crashing his cymbals and drums to ward away evil demons and chanting an endless stream of mantras.

The men and women, with their Tibetan features and beautiful clothes, began to take in the harvest, as I found myself forgetting about the passage of time, and allowed myself to become entranced in a timeless world. I managed to paint a large panorama from the top of the hill above the palace, amidst the prayer flags, hot under the sun and blown by the wind. But for all the drawings and paintings, such a place was so full of what was inspiring and significant that I could barely express a fraction of what I saw and felt. But it was more than this: it was as if I was only just beginning my journey – or beginning to discover what I had set out to find. It seemed to be contained in the simplest of things – stones, a wall or a cairn. The way in which the Ladakhis made these simple things seemed to be connected with the earth itself and with some inner part of us all. The nagging sense of universal significance held within objects like a secret. An inner vision, an ability to see below the surface meaning. The transcendant within the temporal. This is trying to put words to something that is inexpressible, something which I felt and accepted without thinking 'why?' or 'how?' I don't know if it was the mountains, or the temples, or the people with their gentle friendly natures, or the songs they sang in the fields, or even the wind on my face standing on a high point: but I knew I was closer to what fascinated me most. A place where the past tradition and the present moment merge, where even the smallest things are of significance – from the massive mountain flanks and ice peaks, down to the tiny diamonds seen in tufts of grass as the low sun catches each blade in its light.

This was why I had come so far, to experience the feeling of a high, remote and special place, with deep resonances of a spiritual sense or understanding prevalent all around. Now I felt that a connection had been made, one that gave my whole journey a meaning, a sense of consecutiveness, linking Athos, Turkey and Ladakh. This feeling never deserted me, even as I was leaving Ladakh, as the snows came lower down the mountains, and the passes had to be crossed before winter came in.

I went down on the road by which I had come, again on top of a Sikh truck, this time travelling with Michael, whom I had befriended in Leh. He sat reading *Pride and Prejudice* under a brightly coloured umbrella, as the landscape rolled by. The trees had lost many of their leaves and the barley harvest was being brought in from little oval fields. The town of Drass at dawn was diamond bright with a cold wind blowing, everything violet and blue, covered in the golden dust kicked up by the sheep. Freezing nights on top of the truck, then down into Kashmir. The rivers all green and white, fir trees like stilts with their lower branches stripped off, sometimes hung with straw like giant bird's nests. Then back to the chalet houses and the increasingly strong and pungent smells of the lower valleys. As the altitude drops, everything becomes thick and intense. Down in Srinagar, taking the bags from the roof of the truck, back in the maelstrom of Indian life, Ladakh was almost a dream, as if it had happened long ago. I had spent months up in the mountains, following the phases of the moon. It was time to move further east.

66   *The valley of the Indus at Leh, from the north. September 10th 1986*

Tisseru stupa, Leh, being excavated during the barley harvest. September 17th 1986 69

70

Gyaltsen cho

72   *Mount Sumeru, the Buddha and part of the Wheel of Life, from a wall painting in the Sankar Gompa. September 25th 1986*

73

74   *Tikse Gompa in the Leh valley. October 2nd 1986*

78   *The Kastamandap, near Durbar Square, Kathmandu, looking south. November 11th 1986*

80   *Buddhas at the base of Swayambunath, the monkey temple, Kathmandu. November 13th 1986*

81

82

Buddhas halfway up the steps to the stupa, Swayambunath, Kathmandu. November 14th 1986 83

88   *Tashilumpo monastery, Shigatse. November 21st 1986*

89

90   *The Kumbum and monastery, Gyantse. November 24th 1986*

ཅུ་ཁ་རྩེ་རྫ་ལུགས་

92   *Buddha inside the Kumbum, Gyantse. November 25th 1986.*

The Potala, Lhasa, from Chogpori Hill. November 29th 1986   95

Roof of the Jokhang, Lhasa. December 1st 1986   97

বক্রব রুখাশ্বদ

98

The Potala and the roof of the Jokhang at dusk. December 4th 1986   99

102 *The River Kyi Chu to the south of Lhasa, from Chogpori Hill. December 13th 1986*

སྟ་ཡར་ཀླུ་རི

Entrance to the Jokhang, with prostrating pilgrims. December 16th 1986   105

الله اكبر

清真寺

ब'केरि थ्रेट्स

106

" Raj Lakhang "

The mosque in Lhasa. December 19th 1986 107

108   *The Potala from the road to the Norbulinka, the Dalai Lama's summer palace. December 22nd 1986*

109

110   *The Potala and Chogpori Hill from the roof of the Banakshol Hotel. December 23rd 1986*

111

In January I went with some friends to Samye, a small town on the far side of the mountains to the south of Lhasa. There was only one place to stay, kept by an ogress of a Chinese woman, so we dumped our bags there and went back out into the courtyard. A group of Tibetans around a campfire beckoned us over to talk and have tea with them. We sat and exchanged cigarettes and drank a palatable kind of cherry brandy, as the full moon rose through the bare branches of some trees. The Tibetan women forced the men to dance with them, as one of our group, Iaṅ, played his tin whistle. The men were somewhat the worse from the brandy but we all managed to mimic vague motions with our arms and legs in the moonlit square – the Tibetans laughing at the sight of my long-sleeved chuba swinging in the air. It was a magical time for us all, just the few of us in this quiet empty square, with the doors of the gompa standing mysterious and dark behind us.

The next day I entered the monastery. It proved to have some of the most beautiful wall paintings I had ever seen. They had been badly defaced – in some the eyes of the Buddha had been gouged out; others were severely splashed with concrete from the cement-mixers used in the restoration work. Still, there survived many large figures of the Buddha, each one subtly different, surrounded by different sorts of flowers or lotus blossoms, each petal exquisitely executed. Between these figures the spaces were filled with stories from former lives of the Buddha.

I had seen paintings of a similar kind in Lhasa but these seemed to be older and of a higher quality. There was also a poignancy to the beauty of what remained here. To climb over woodstacks amid the dirt and the dust and peer at a high corner of an unknown, humble and yet supreme piece of devotional painting meant more to me than to study a beautifully preserved masterpiece in a museum.

The fruits of the teachings of the East are visible in these images as in the lives of the people. They are by painters working without the need for personal expression, who had produced work expressing an inner world of eternal truth, beyond problems and desires. Just as in Byzantine icons, and in the Muslim and Hindu images, it scarcely matters that a style might stop developing, since the paintings indicate a truth that transcends time and space. The images are merely stepping stones, indicating in material form something that by its very nature is formless and timeless.

In the same way, it seems that the differences between religious art-forms are unimportant too. How to express the inexpressible? Yet these painters and builders and sculptors had managed to indicate it in their different ways, through the power of their faith and their inherent sense of spiritual significance. You can see it in the lives of the people on this journey – the monks' devotions on Athos, the Muslims along the road praying to Allah, the Hindu women at the shrines of Ganesh and Shiva, the prostrators at the doors of the Jokhang in Lhasa. It hardly matters that the objects of their devotions often become unreadable – the soot-stained icons wrapped in silver, the crumbling red slabs of Ganesh, the hidden wrathful deities in Ladakh, too terrible to reveal to the unwary visitor – it is in the hearts of the people that the significance of these material forms lies. And I felt that the painters of Samye too had locked this like a secret into the very lines and shading of each lotus-petal on the wall . . .

Once back in Lhasa, I paid a visit to the Sky Burial site north of the city. I had avoided it before, not wanting to interfere or offend, but in the afternoon, after any possible burial had taken place, I walked up the long straight road leading out past the black drogpa tents on the flat open floor of the valley, and across a wasteland dotted with the drying carcasses of yaks. At the base of the stony hills stands the massive stone on which the bodies are cut up and fed to the vultures. The clothes of the deceased littered the ground at its foot and a monk sat intoning mantras and blowing his thigh-bone horn. Despite its purpose, it was not a morbid or depressing place. The wind blew inexorably across the plain and the sun shone crisply on even the most distant of points. The monks prayed for the benefit of the dead and of all sentient beings. A group of Tibetans arrived, underwent a small ceremony and then sat around joking and drinking tea, having come to terms in some way with their own approaching death. As the sun drops lower in the sky, the burial site falls under the shadow of a nearby ridge. I climbed up, and on top there is a wide view of the whole Lhasa valley. Following the ridge still higher, there emerged, unseen before, a large figure of the Buddha, standing above the valley, above the city, above the place of the dead, with a gesture almost of benediction, silently testifying to a truth and a knowledge beyond death itself.

After the sun had set, and the moon rose, I could see below me the moonlight reflecting off water, where before there had been a dry parched wasteland. A river from the day's snow-melt had formed in the valley, a natural barrier, appearing every evening, gone by the morning, between the city and the place of the dead. It was a long walk back into Lhasa.

114   *Meru Gompa, Lhasa, with pilgrims from Amdo, eastern Tibet. Christmas Day 1986*

ཕྲ་ཅི་ལྷ་ཁང་།

115

116   *The Jokhang from roof of The Mendzekhang. January 12th 1987*

Samye, the oldest Buddhist monastery in Tibet. January 16th 1987

120   *Rooftop of the Potala. January 20th 1987*

བོ་ད་ལ་

122   *Sky Burial site, north of Lhasa. January 22nd 1987*

123

124   *Stone-carved Buddha on the ridge above the Sky Burial site. January 22nd 1987*

Notes on the Paintings

12–13 *Mount Athos* from the capital, Karyes. The peninsula has been a self-governing monastic community at least since the ninth century and remains as one of the few centres of Byzantine Orthodox Christian monasticism.

14–15 The church of the *Protaton* in *Karyes* was built in the first half of the tenth century. The paintings are by Manuel Panselinos, chief representative of the Macedonian School, at the beginning of the fourteenth century. The 'iconostasis' is a partition separating the sanctuary from the main body of the church, usually painted with icons in a traditional order.

16–17 The entrance to the monastery of *Stavronikita*, the smallest of the twenty Athonite monasteries, showing the vine trellis and aqueduct.

18–19 *Karakallou*, built in the eleventh century. On the left is the hoist by which grain is lifted into the monastery tower. Below, the church, in typical Byzantine style, occupies the middle of the courtyard. On the left-hand side are the balconies of the visitors' quarters.

20–21 *Cross* and *Hesychasterion* or hermitage, a small hut used by monks who seek complete asceticism and solitude. They are surrounded by ravines and cliffs, and access is only possible by steep paths.

22–23 Monastery of *Dionyssiou*, built in 1370–1374. The mural paintings, showing precise details of many events in the Book of Revelation, Chapters 6, 7 and 8, are by Tzorzis, 1546–7, of the Cretan School.

24–25 *Panteleimonos*, seen from the roof-top beside the bell-tower. The monastery is eighteenth-century; during the nineteenth century 1,000 Russian monks lived here; now there are only a few left.

26–27 The monastery of *Dochiariou* was built in the tenth century. Like most of the Athonite monasteries its church almost fills the quadrangle of the monks' quarters.

30–31 *Istanbul* from *Galata Bridge* across the Golden Horn. The mosque at the end of the bridge is Yeni Camii (the New Mosque) and the one on the right-hand edge of the picture is Suleimanye Camii. The Blue Mosque (Sultanahmet) occupies the highest point on the horizon to the left of the bridge; Agia Sophia is to the left of that, beyond the plume of smoke from the steamer.

32–33 *Istanbul from my hotel window.* Agia Sophia, on the left, was built in AD 537, during the reign of Justinian, and was originally the Christian heart of Byzantine Constantinople. The Blue Mosque on the right was built over a thousand years later, 1608–14.

34–35 *Topkapi Palace, Istanbul*, painted from the Ottoman Sultan's private quarters. The harem occupied the striped buildings to the right. The fat tower of the university dominates the far skyline.

36–37 *Mardin*, looking south towards the Syrian plain from the path leading to the citadel above the town, with the domes of the Sultan Isa Madrasa immediately below, built in 1385 (and now housing a museum and school). Further down to the right are the minaret and dome of Ulu Camii – both Seljuk in style. The town was once a crucial crossroads of trade routes, governed in successive periods by the Romans, Byzantines, Arabs, Kurds, Seljuks and Arturkid Turkomen. Mardin resisted Saladin but fell to Tamerlane in the fourteenth-century Mongol invasion.

38–39 *Mar Gabriel*, Syriac Orthodox Monastery, built AD 397. There were eighty Orthodox monasteries in this part of eastern Turkey in the Middle Ages. Mar Gabriel is one of the few now remaining. There are both monks and nuns here under a Bishop, and about thirty boys from the surrounding villages. The services are in Aramaic, the language of Jesus.

40–41 The landscape around *Mar Gabriel* at dusk. In the foreground are the onions and cabbages of the monastery garden and the tomb of Egyptian Coptic Christians.

42–43 *Akdamar* – the church of the Holy Cross. Armenian tenth-century (AD 915–921). The outside of the church is decorated with extraordinary carvings illustrating stories from the Bible. Inside are the remains of Byzantine wall-paintings. Because Lake Van has no natural outflow and the only way for water to escape is by evaporation, it is heavily alkaline and thick with soda. The water is buoyant and bathing here is like swimming in silk.

44–45 *Mount Ararat* from *Doğubeyazit*. The volcano where Noah's Ark came to rest (Genesis Chapter 8, verse 4) is Turkey's highest mountain, considered the centre of the world by Armenians and the roof of the world by the Arabs. It is 35 kilometres from the Iranian border.

46–47 The vegetable market in *Peshawar*, Pakistan. Potatoes are being sold in the Old Bazaar. On the right is a group of Afghan refugees.

48–49 *Badshahi Mosque*, Lahore, Pakistan, built in 1673–74, during the reign of Aurangzeb. 10,000 people can be accommodated in the courtyard.

52–53 Dal Lake, from the Hindu Temple, *Srinagar* – close to where William Carpenter painted his panorama in the nineteenth century, now in the Victoria & Albert Museum, London. The citadel on the high ground at the left and Golden Island to the right are both visible.

54–55 *Buddha* on rock face, Leh, Ladakh. Tsemo Gompa is above, on the ridge. The 'touching earth' gesture of the Shakyamuni Buddha symbolises the truth of the teaching, calling the earth as His witness.

56–57 *Tsemo Gompa* and prayer flags. Sixteenth-century gompa, the remains of a much larger complex of buildings now long disappeared, above the town of Leh.

58–59 Kitchen of the *Palace View Kidar Hotel*, Leh. A kindly old lady who runs the hotel is baking bread in the oven, with the tall, brass-banded butter-tea churns standing on the left-hand side at the back. The brass jugs and pots in the alcoves on the far wall are family heirlooms. A deservedly popular place to stay.

60–61 Interior of the *Shrine Room, Royal Palace, Leh*. The walls are lined with books of Buddhist scriptures. Demon Yamantaka masks hang from the pillars used in ritual dances. The central skylight is typical of Tibetan gompa architecture.

62–63 *The Royal Palace*, Leh, was built in the seventeenth century, at about the same time as the Potala in Lhasa.

66–67 The valley of the *Indus at Leh*, from a ridge to the north. The cairns are reminiscent of the pre-Buddhist Bon-po religion, a shamanistic animism which was replaced by Buddhism here in the seventh and eighth centuries.
68–69 *Tisseru stupa*, Leh, is said to contain relics of the Buddha. The Indian Government was excavating it when I was there. The barley field below it had been cleared by the time I had painted the picture.
70–71 Antechamber of *Sankar Gompa*, three kilometres north of Leh. On the far wall the Wheel of Life – one of the oldest of Buddhist images – depicts, like a mirror, earthly life. In the centre is the Ego (cock-pride, pig-lust, snake-hate) and the Six States: Heaven, Hell, Animals, People, Titans and Pretas (hungry ghosts). Around it is the Cycle of Dependent Origination, which the Buddha calls on us to escape. To the left is a schematic map of the world – seven rings of seven mountains, dominated by Mount Sumeru. Golstan Cho was a monk attending the monastery who kindly modelled for me.
72–73 *The Buddha* outside the Wheel of Life, from a wall painting in Sankar Gompar. The hand of Yama holds the Wheel of Life. On the wheel itself, two details of the Cycle – a man carrying a dead body and a woman giving birth. To the left of the Buddha is a representation of Mount Sumeru.
74–75 *Tikse Gompa* was built in the mid fifteenth century on a steep rock beside the Indus river, farther upstream than Leh. The gompa is on the top, with the monks' living quarters lower down the slope.
78–79 *The Kastamandap*, Kathmandu. A rest-house for pilgrims, a shrine, and a market area beneath its eaves. Said to have been built from a single tree. It is constructed over the crossroads that mark the original centre of Kathmandu.
80–81 *Buddhas* at the base of Swayambunath, to the west of Kathmandu. The Dhyani (meditation) Buddha Aksobhaya, touches the earth, symbolising the unshakeable, steadfast nature of the teaching, like the earth.
82–83 *Buddhas* halfway up the steps to the stupa, Swayambunath, Kathmandu.
84–85 *The stupa*, Swayambunath, Kathmandu.

Said to be one of the places where the Buddha preached. Earliest evidence of a shrine here is from AD 250, but the oldest surviving structures date from the seventh century.
88–89 *Tashilumpo monastery*, Shigatse. The seat of the Panchen Lama, founded 1447, once had 4,000 monks in it. The large white wall on the left was used for hanging giant thang'kas, the religious cloth-paintings. The red building houses a huge figure of Maitreya, the future Buddha, 86-feet high. The palace of the Panchen Lamas is in the centre.
90–91 *The Kumbum and gompa*, Gyantse. The largest stupa in Tibet was built in 1427. The monastery dates from 1365 and once housed 1,000 monks. There were several other monastic buildings identical to the central one, flanking it, which were destroyed by the Chinese.
92–93 *Buddha* inside the Kumbum, Gyantse. The Dhyani Buddha Amoghasiddhi, symbolising the 'all-accomplishing wisdom' and the path of action and involvement in the world. The gesture of fearlessness.
94–95 *The Potala*, Lhasa, from Chogpori, or 'Medicine', Hill. The Potala was founded by Songtsen Gampo in the seventh century. The present building was built by the fifth Dalai Lama between 1643 and 1693 and has been added to by many subsequent Dalai Lamas. The religious buildings are painted red; the secular white.
96–97 *Roof of the Jokhang*, Lhasa. The great temple in Lhasa was founded in the seventh century by Songtsen Gampo to house the figures of the Buddha brought by his two wives from China and Nepal.
98–99 *The Potala* and the roof of the Jokhang at dusk.
102–103 *The River Kyi Chu* to the south of Lhasa, from Chogpori Hill. Samye is on the far side of these mountains.
104–105 *Doors of the Jokhang*. Tibetan pilgrims travel hundreds of miles to pay their respects to the holiest shrine of Tibet Buddhism. It is the spiritual heart of Tibet. Most of the pilgrims will make 108 full body prostrations, an auspicious number.
106–107 *The mosque* in Lhasa. Muslims from Ladakh and Xinjiang have lived in Lhasa and

Tibet for hundreds of years. The building is a unique blend of Islamic, Tibetan and Chinese design.
108–109 *The Potala* from the road to the Norbulinka, the Dalai Lama's summer palace.
110–111 *The Potala* and 'Happiness Road', the east end of the road running through Lhasa. The Friendship Store and Muslim tea-houses are to the right; the old town to the left.
114–115 *Meru Gompa*, at the end of a tight alley in Lhasa. The women are pilgrims from Amdo, in eastern Tibet, resting beside the juniper burner on a freezing day in December. The doorway was being repainted. Chicken and sheep and lots of ice.
116–117 *Jokhang* from the roof of the *Mendzekhang* showing the changes to the front of the gompa made by the Chinese. They cleared away the buildings to form a square. This is the place where the Khampas – warrior-tradesmen from eastern Tibet – drogpas, pilgrims, tourists and off-duty Chinese soldiers all congregate – the scene of recent troubles. My friend Chris was shot in the shoulder by Chinese firing into the crowds. Juniper burners and old stone pillars are visible. This is the beginning and end of the Barkhor pilgrim circuit or 'chora'.
118–119 *Samye*. Tibet's first monastery, the site of Padmasambhara's introduction of Buddhism into Tibet. Built by Trisong Detsan in AD 779. The town is a mandala in plan, with the gompa in the centre.
120–121 Roof of the *Potala*. The roofs were built by the fifth and seventh Dalai Lamas. The knot symbol in the awnings is one of eight auspicious symbols of Tibetan Buddhism, symbolising the unity of all things and the illusory nature of time.
122–123 *Sky Burial site*. Ritual burials in Tibet are based on the elements – earth, air, fire and water. Sky burials are partly practical. There is little suitable earth in Tibet to bury in – it is too stony and often frozen. The body is broken up on the stone and fed to vultures – a return to the air.
124–125 Amoghasiddhi *Buddha* above the Sky Burial site. Like the Buddha in the Kumbum, Gyantse (pp. 92–93), this Buddha makes the gesture of fearlessness.

Dedication

The Tibetans have few voices in their defence and are scarcely able to preserve
what little of their cultural heritage now survives.

It is my hope that the paintings in this book which record some of
the Tibetan richness that does remain can draw attention to
their terrible plight under Chinese rule.

If the world continues to turn a blind eye to Tibet she will
almost certainly become no more than a colony for the expanding population of China,
resulting in degradation and dehumanisation for the Tibetans themselves.

Considering how kind and open the Tibetans were to a complete stranger,
showing me such generosity and humour despite their hardships,
it is with horror and pain that I hear of more deaths in Tibet –
probably including the death of people who were personally kind to me.

This book is dedicated to the Tibetans, and to all those people that helped me along
the way, who showed me such patience, generosity, understanding and good humour.

May 1989

Acknowledgments

Anyone familiar with overland travel in Asia will realise that almost nothing is said in this book of the noise, discomforts, uncertainties and sickness that are an integral part of any journey like this. Nor of the changes in the speed of life, the slow absorption into a different way of seeing things, nor the thousands of incidental aspects of everyday life that are so fascinating – the boy musicians on the buses in Turkey, the incense and 'bidi' sellers in India and the roadside chai-stalls . . . For this, my only excuse is lack of space. For the same reason, many people who helped me and who in various ways became part of my journey have not yet been mentioned. These are:

Carol and Soteris Kakouli; Ina Argiriou and Fofi; Olivier Methou; the monk in Dochiariou; Sinan in Istanbul; Özcan Aslan and Chihat in Urfa; everyone in the Yildiz Otel, Mardin; Malphono Isa and all at Mar Gabriel for their hospitality and kindness; Shirzad in Tabriz; Khan in Baluchistan; Alberto and Gary in Lahore; Scott Smith; Vicky; Peter Arndt; Clayton Spitzer and Jim; Vincent 'the Good'; Richard Shenfield; Helena Norberg-Hodge and John Page; Nawang and Chandol of Changspa; Ian Worrall and Tashi; Gregg McCarthy and Gary 'Ganesh 501'; the Sayamis in Kathmandu; Chris Gamm and Kerry Moran; Martha, Vicky, Priscilla and Betsy; Andrew Fox; Krishna at Kuldi Ghar; the Magician; Maria;

Lance; Jaida N'a Sandra; Jamyang; Heather Berns; John Sevcik and Hua; Adrian Gilboe; Westy; Paul Ingleman; Adrian Moon; Gunnar Herbert; and Janice Sandeen.

Special thanks to Michael Murray, Jim Rogers, Russell Johnson and Barbara Ieralli, for being such good friends. I shall always treasure our times together.

Also to Robin Broadbank, Pip Belfield, Keith Patterson, June Osborne and Paul Goulding, Giuliano Ferrari, Carl Magnusson, Kim Marsland, Charles Shearer, Adam Nicolson, Robert Sackville West and John Meek.